YOUR KNOWLEDGE HAS VALUE

Bibliographic information published by the German National Library:

The German National Library lists this publication in the National Bibliography; detailed bibliographic data are available on the Internet at http://dnb.dnb.de .

Imprint:

Copyright © 2017 GRIN Verlag, Open Publishing GmbH
Print and binding: Books on Demand GmbH, Norderstedt Germany
ISBN: 9783668470996

This book at GRIN:

http://www.grin.com/en/e-book/368352/a-rural-primary-care-provider-adherence-to-the-ada-guideline-for-frequency

Leonard Kahungu

A rural Primary Care Provider Adherence to the ADA Guideline for Frequency of A1c Testing

GRIN Publishing

GRIN - Your knowledge has value

Since its foundation in 1998, GRIN has specialized in publishing academic texts by students, college teachers and other academics as e-book and printed book. The website www.grin.com is an ideal platform for presenting term papers, final papers, scientific essays, dissertations and specialist books.

Visit us on the internet:

http://www.grin.com/

http://www.facebook.com/grincom

http://www.twitter.com/grin_com

A rural Primary Care Provider Adherence to the ADA Guideline for Frequency of A1c Testing

Leonard Kahungu

Theory of Prevention as Intervention and Neuman's Systems Model 3

Author 3

Purpose..4

Relevant Major Assumptions...4

Major Concepts..5

Theoretical Framework: The Adherence-to-Awareness Model 6

Rationale for Selecting the Theory of Prevention as Intervention and NSM 7

Rationale for Selecting the Adherence-to-Awareness Model...7

References..11

A rural Primary Care Provider Adherence to the ADA Guideline for Frequency of A1c Testing.

Diabetes mellitus (DM) is worldwide epidemic and is the leading cause of poor health, physical disabilities and premature death. Globally, 422 million people were diagnosed with diabetes in 2014, and over 1.5 million people died from diabetes-related complications (World Health Organization, 2016). In the United States (U.S.), diabetes was the cause of over 74.9 thousand deaths and 1.85 million disability years lived in 2013. The widespread presence rate of type 2 diabetes (T2DM) in the U.S. is estimated to reach 44 million by 2034. Presently, nearly 25.8 million adults and children have diabetes, with T2DM being more prevalent in Latinos, African Americans, Asian Americans, Native Americans, other Pacific Islanders and Native Hawaiians (World Health Organization, 2016).

Purpose

The purpose of this scholarly project is to examine the effects of motivational interviewing (MI), on T2DM patient adherence to A1c testing.

PICO

The overarching research question for this scholarly project is as follows: In adult patients (18 years and older) with T2DM located in a southern Mississippi outpatient setting, what are the effects (if any) of motivational interviewing on patients' adherence to recommended A1c testing?

Theory of Prevention as Intervention and Neuman's Systems Model

The Neuman's Systems Model presents a wide-ranging holistic and system-centered approach that is made up of flexibility elements. The primary focus on the model is based on patient's response to potential or actual environmental stressors. It utilizes the primary, secondary and tertiary nursing prevention interventions, which seek to retain, attain or maintain the wellness of the patient's system wellness (Gigliotti, 2012). Thus, the theory of Prevention as Intervention is one of the major middle-range theories derived the Neuman's System Model (NSM) of nursing.

Author

The NSM model was first coined by Betty Neuman and subsequently introduced in nursing practice and education in 1970s. Betty Neuman was born in Lowel, Ohio in 1924 and obtained her first Bachelor of Science in Nursing in 1957. In 1966, Neuman received her master's degree in Mental Health Public Health Consultation in 1966 from UCLA. In addition, Betty Neuman attained her doctoral degree in Clinical Psychology in 1985, from pacific Western University. It is during this period that she started working towards incorporating nursing practice in mental health (Neuman, 2002).

Consequently, the Neuman's System Model was first published in 1972 as "A Model for Teaching Total Person Approach to Patient Problems in Nursing Research. The primary aim of the first publication was to facilitate the formulation of nursing education program that would allow the students to understand nursing problems, from a detailed perspective. NSM was then published in Conceptual Models for Nursing Practice as a first edition in 1974 and the second edition in 1980 (Fawcett & Desanto-Madeya, 2013).

As previously mentioned, the theory of prevention as intervention is derived from NSM; hence the authorship is widely credited to Betty Neuman. As a result, the theory flows and is structurally consistent with the Neuman's System Model. The theory proposes that the patient's system is the primary objective for nursing is to improve the optimal stability of the client by preventing or intervening to give support (Neuman, 1989). Prevention as intervention is defined as the process utilized by nurses to provide appropriate care so as to achieve the objective of the stability of the patient. Therefore, intervention can start at any stage or point, when the stressor is suspected or isolated (Fawcett & Desanto-Madeya, 2013).

Purpose

The holistic goal of nursing, as defined by the NSM, is to improve the optimal stability of patient's system by preventing stress of intervening to provide required support. Similarly, the purpose of the theory of prevention as intervention is to avert any form of diseases or problems prior to medical involvement. Prevention as intervention can be achieved through three levels, in efforts to restore the patient's stability, in the absence of stressors (Neuman, 2002).

Relevant Major Assumptions

- Each patient has a unique system that is characterized with complex factors and attributed within a range of responses limited in a basic structure.
- There are numerous stressors that are universal, and each stressor may have different implications on the normal stability of the patient.
- Each client has developed a normal range of reactions to the environment known as the normal line of defense. The normal line of defense can be used as a standard in measuring health deviation of a patient.
- The specific inter-relationship of client variables can at any given period, interfere with the extent to which the patient is protected by the flexible line of defense against potential stress reactions.
- When the flexible line of defense fails to protect the patient's system against the environmental stressors, they break through the line of defense.
- The patient is a dynamic compound of the inter-relationships of the variables, regardless of the state of a disease or wellness. Thus, wellness is often in a continuum of available energy to sustain the patient's system to achieve desired stability.
- Patients have hidden internal resistance elements, also known as line of resistance. The line of resistance plays a central role in stabilizing and realigning the patient to restore the usual state of wellness.
- The primary prevention is utilized in patient assessment and intervention, in isolation and reduction of potential or specific risk factors.
- The secondary prevention is often concerned with the symptomatology after a reaction to environmental stressors, suitable ranking of intervention main concerns along with treatment plans aimed at reducing their harmful impacts.

- Tertiary prevention intervention is concerned to transformational process taking place as reconstruction process takes starts, and the repairing factors move them back in a cycle that leads to primary intervention.
- The patient is in dynamic and continuous energy exchange with the surroundings

Major Concepts

According to Neuman, the variables of the client in interaction with the external and internal surroundings make up the system of a person. The NSM has four major variables of the patient are psychological, developmental, spiritual, social-cultural and physiological. The theory also highlights different concepts, including the degree of reaction, wellness, stressors, open system, basic structure as well as the intervention (Neuman, 1974). Prevention as a nursing intervention focuses on ensuring that the stressors and the reactions as a result of external and internal environmental factors do not have adverse effects on the system balance of a person. An individual is normally viewed as an open system that communicates with internal and external stressors. A person is exposed to constant and steady changes towards a vibrant state of system permanence or towards disease of various grades (Moss et al. 2002). The environment is a paramount field that is connected to the system and its purpose.

Neuman's theory has two perspectives, the one that affects and is affected by the system. The internal environment is found inside the system of a person. It accounts for factors that influence the system of the client within the boundaries. The external environment is based or found outside the client's system. Neuman defines health as the degree of system's stability and it ranges from wellness to sickness. When the optimum needs of the system are met, then optimal wellness is achieved, while the absence or failure to meet the needs of the system, then the illness is observed. Subsequently, the death of a system (client) is occurs when the energy required to sustain life is not availed on time (Mazroui et al. 2009). As a result, the primary of nursing is to establish the appropriate interventions when the patient's system is not balanced as a result of either internal or external stressors (Neuman, 1989).

Nursing interventions are mainly based at supporting the system so as to allow it adjust, maintain, restore or take any direction to achieve stability of various variables and internal or external stressors, with a primary aim of conserving the energy. An open system is defined as an uninterrupted flow of input and process, output and response (Parker & Smith, 2012). The flexible line of defense is a protective mechanism which surrounds and protects the normal line from invasion from stressors. Normal line of defense, on the other hand, tends to develop with time and considered normal for a certain system. It also becomes standard for wellness-deviance determination (Mazroui, 2009). The lines of resistance are protection factors that are activated when stressors have bypassed the normal line of defense, resulting to reactionary or precautionary measures. Routinely, prevention as an intervention strategy is utilized when internal or external stressors have not infiltrated the standard line of defense (Neuman, 1974).

Theoretical Framework: The Adherence-to-Awareness Model

Pathman et al. (1996) first utilized non-adherence to national principles for childhood immunizations as a model to formulate a conceptual framework to deal with non-adherence to recommended guidelines. In the adherence-to-awareness model, Pathman et al. described the sequential, cognitive along with behavioral phases required to accomplish physician observance to guidelines as awareness, adoption and adherence. With regards to awareness, physicians are compelled to understand the existence of the guidelines, making the dissemination process of the guidelines very fundamental. Agreement requires health practitioners to agree with the accuracy and dependability of the provided guidelines. Failure to agree with the recommended guidelines leads to the freezing of the treatment process.

Even though physicians may be pressured to adopt the guidelines as a result of peer pressure and possible malpractice litigations, Pathman speculates that most physicians develop the tendency of using guidelines in their treatment plans because they are aware of it and agree with the importance of using the recommended standards in promoting and maintaining patients' wellbeing. Pathmam et al. further appreciates that adoption and adherence are rampant in evidence-based practice, particularly because of the increases scrutiny from the health regulatory organizations and insurance providers. However, Pathman et al. proposes that physicians are engaged in voluntary compliance of the appropriate guidelines in the provision of care, mainly because they are aware the importance of such conduct in the health care practice.

The adherence-to-awareness model was further developed by Cabana et al. (1999), improving its scope to produce multi-directional flow which emulates the cognitive conflict that lead to barriers manifested as physician non-adherence to required standards. Specific concepts expanded by Cabana et al. (1999) includes lack of knowledge such as lack of awareness and familiarity; attitudes regarding appropriate standards such as lack of agreement, self-efficacy, and outcome expectancy as well as inertia of traditional practice; while the final notion is the behavior which is characterized by external barriers.

Rationale for Selecting the Theory of Prevention as Intervention and NSM

The NSM provided framework to guide this DNP project in improving the quality of life and the outcomes of therapeutic interventions among diabetic clients. In the study, the client was an individual diagnosed with type-2 diabetes. Since all the clients have diabetes, they had passed the asymptomatic stage that requires primary intervention and required either secondary or tertiary prevention (Mazroui, 2009). Therefore, the environmental stressors and the internal phathophysiology extra-personal and intrapersonal stress factors had passed through the normal lines of defense and perhaps the flexible lines of defense. The variations are brought about by differences in severity of signs and symptoms and the state of the diseases. This DNP study proposes the utilization of the NSM and the theory of prevention to discover appropriate strategies along with programs that have the capacity to improve the control or management of stressors related t diabetes.

Typically, the conceptual framework as presented by the NSM and the theory of prevention as intervention seeks to strengthen the line of resistance and lessen the effects of diabetic stressors on the client. Using the NSM and the theory of prevention as intervention, the health practitioners can act or take appropriate measures to protect patients suffering from T2DM from negative effects of diabetic stressors. The normal and flexible lines of defenses can also be strengthened to protect the patients from developing complication associated with diabetes as a result of environmental stressors. Malijanian et al. (2002) utilized the NSM conceptual framework to complete their studies on how to improve the diabetes management through provider-based disease management program.

Rationale for Selecting the Adherence-to-Awareness Model

Whereas type 2 diabetes cannot be cured, there are several ways in which the complications can be managed to improve the quality of life and prevent the development of various diseases. Besides, type-2 diabetes can be prevented by adopting effective lifestyles. Consequently, the American Diabetes Association (ADA) has developed therapeutic tool that provides appropriate standards to facilitate the management of T2DM. In other words, ADA provides standard procedures that ought to be followed when handling diabetic patients. Regrettably, studies conducted via the US National Ambulatory Medical Care Survey illustrates only 27% patients diagnosed with complication resulting from T2DM are directed to take A1c testing (Neumiller et al. 2010)

The DNP capstone quality enhancement project aims at improving nursing practitioners' adherence to the ADA standards that require all patients suffering from T2DM to undertake A1c testing. In particular, this project will employ the adherence-to-awareness conceptual framework to develop the knowledge of the nurse practitioners on the importance of undertaking A1c tests (awareness), educate them on how the A1c can be used to inform clinical treatment plans (agreement), and how to integrate A1c value on the patients' education to improve the patient's ability and awareness of the significance of glycemic control (adoption). Therefore, the adherence-to-awareness model was selected so as to inform the DNP project regarding the lack of awareness, attitudes, which could result to lack of agreement, behaviors and other factors that could hinder the adherence to the ADA guidelines when dealing with diabetic patients.

Pathman et al. (1996) proposes that the primary step towards adherence is the understanding of guidelines. Normally, nurse practitioners are educated on how to manage T2DM and other ailments, as required by the nursing education curriculum in the U.S. Additionally, ADA and other concerned bodies provide freely accessible guidelines on how to manage diabetes to avert the risk of developing affiliated complications. Evidently, lack of adherence is widely caused by lack of knowledge regarding the relevant guidelines and their goals. Consequently, Glasser (2010) explores low ADA adherence rate, where the findings illustrates only 21% of the sampled population recorded A1c value in a period of two years.

In their studies, McClellan et al. (2003) also agreed with Glasser (2010) and propose that dissemination of information regarding the objectives and existence of ADA guidelines could be enhanced through educational programs in billings sent to the care providers in Medicaid and Medicare Services. While employing the adherence-to-awareness tool, Delaronde (2005) established that only 38.1% of the participants stated that their physicians did not inform them the importance of undertaking at least two A1c tests on annual basis, while 33.3% declared that they have never heard of the A1c tests. These results further support a study conducted by Neumiller et al (2010) as previously cited.

Studies completed by Schafer (2006) and Parcero et al. (2011) indicates that adherence to ADA guidelines improves glycemic management and reduces the prevalence of complications associated with T2DM. Nevertheless, lack of self-efficacy of the nurse practitioners leads to clinical inertia, which is defined as unwillingness or incapability to strengthen medication therapeutic in patients suffering from non-therapeutic glycemic control. Schaefer (2006) defines clinical inertia as the inability of the care providers to advice on the required medication practices necessary to maintain Alc levels. Furthermore, Cabana et al. (1999) describes clinical inertia as barriers related to the attitude of the providers and are directly linked to self efficacy.

Figure 1: Pathman et al. 1996 Model

Researches completed by Khoong et al. (2014), Massey et al. (2010), Parcero (2011), Siminero (2005) and Heisler et al. (2005) affirm that physician agreement with the guideline is important in the full adoption of guidelines. Thus adoption and full acknowledgement of the ADA guidelines concerning Alc tests among the physicians is fundamental in the evaluation of glycemic index and the enhancement of glycemic control among the patients. This is attributed to the fact that physicians utilize Alc tests to advice the patients on their diets, recommend appropriate physical exercises and the intensification of diabetic management practices and medication. Moreover, care providers who understand and adhere to ADA guidelines are more likely to engage on holistic approaches to reach the patients though community proxies to promote community health interventions (Massey, 2010).

Report done by Davis et al. (2014) found out that only 21% of patient with optimal Alc intensified their treatment. This indicates that patients who know their Alc through their health practitioners are in a better position to manage their diabetic conditions. Vigersky (2011) also found out that inadequate self efficacy dragged the appropriate application of effective diabetic management practices. The results obtained from Davis et al. (2014) and Vigersky (2011) provides additional evidence that untimely Alc tests delays the commencement of diabetes therapeutic procedures.

Apparently, historical and contemporary studies reveal a pattern where of lack of adherence to the ADA guidelines concerning the effective Alc testing in diabetic management. In addition, evidence reveals that the rate of morbidity and mortality among patients with poor glycemic management practices is relatively high. Therefore, it is the primary reason why this DNP capstone project used the adherence-to-awareness model by Pathman et al. (1996) and Cabana et al (1999).

References

Cabana, M., Rand, C., Powe, N., Wu, A., Wilson, M., Abboud, P, & Rubin, H. (1999). Why
don't physicians follow clinical practice guidelines? *Journal of the American Medical
Association, 282* (15) 1458-1465.

Davis, J., Chavez, B., & Juarez, D. (2014). Adjustments to diabetes medications in response
to increases in Hemoglobin A1c: An epidemiologic study *Journal of
Pharmacotherapy*
48(1) 41-47. Delaronde, S. (2005). Barriers to A1C testing among a managed care
population. *The Diabetes
Educator, 31* (2) 235-239.

Fawcett, J., & Desanto-Madeya, S. (2013). *Contemporary nursing knowledge: Analysis and
evaluation of nursing models and theories.*

Glasser, M., Peters, K., Warner, J., Burkholder, P., Sharp, L., & McGee, B. (2010).
Characteristics of diabetes patients and adherence to standards of care in rural primary
care clinics *Journal of Clinical Outcomes Management 17*(8) 357-361.

Gigliotti, E. (2012). Honoring Dr. Betty Neuman's Contributions to Nursing Science. *Nursing
Science Quarterly, 25,* 4, 297-299.

Koong, E., Gibbert, W., Garbutt, J., Sumner, W., & Brownson, R.(2013). Rural, suburban,
and urban differences in factors that impact physician adherence to clinical preventive
service guidelines *The Journal of Rural Health 30*(7-16).

Massey, C., Appel, S., Buchanan, K., & Cherrington, A. (2010). Improving diabetes care in
rural communities: An overview of current initiatives and a call for renewed efforts.
*Clinical
Diabetes(28)* 20-27.

Mazroui, N., Kamal, M., Ghabash, N., Yacout, T., Kole, P., & McEnlay, J. (2009). Influence
of pharmaceutical care on health outcomes with Type 2 diabetes mellitus. *British
Journal of Clinical Pharmacology, 65*(5), 547-557.

McClellan, W., Millman, L., Presley, R., Couzins, J., & Flanders, W. (2003). Improved
diabetes care by primary care physicians: Results of a group randomized evaluation of
the Medicare health care quality improvement program(HCQIP). *Journal of Clinical
Epidemiology 56*:1210-1217.

Moss-Morris, R., Weinman, J., Petrie, K., Horne, R., Cameron, L., & Buick, D. (2002). The
revised Illness Perception Questionnaire (IPQ-R). *Psychology and Health 17*(7), 1-16.

Malijanian, R., Grey, N., Staff, I., & Aponte, M. (2002). Improved diabetes control through a
    provider-based disease management program. *Disease Management &
    Health Outcomes, 10*(2), 1-8.

Neuman, B. (2002).The Neuman systems model. In B. Neuman & J. Fawcett (Eds.), *The
    Neuman systems model* (4th ed., pp. 3–33). Upper Saddle River, NJ: Prentice Hall.

Neuman, B. (1974). The Betty Neuman health care systems model: A total person approach
    to patient problems. In Riehl, J. & Roy, C. (Eds.), *Conceptual models
    for nursing practice* (pp. 99-134). New York: Appleton-Century-Crofts.

Neuman, B. (1989). *The Neuman Systems Model* (2nd ed.). Norwalk, CT: Appleton &
    Lange.

Neumiller, J., Sclar, D., Robison, L., Maldonado, A., Setter, S. & Skaer, T. (2010)
    Ethnicity/race and the extent of physician-ordered hemoglobin A1c during US office
    based visits by patients with diabetes mellitus [Peer commentary] *The Diabetes
    Educator 36*(1) 65-66.

Parker, M. E., & Smith, M. C. (2010). *Nursing Theories & Nursing Practice*. Philadelphia:
    F.A. Davis Co

Parcero, A., Yaeger, T., Bienkowski, R. (2011). Frequency of monitoring hemoglobin A1C
    and achieving diabetes control, *Journal of Primary Care & Community Health, 2*(3)
    205-208.

Pathman, D., Konrad, T., Freed, G., Freeman, G., & Koch, G. (1996). The awareness-to -
    adherence model of the steps to clinical guideline compliance: The case of pediatric
    vaccine recommendations. *Medical Care, 34*(9) 873-889.

Siminerio, L., Piatt, G., & Zgibor, J. (2005). Implementing the chronic care model for
    improvements in diabetes care and education in a rural primary care practice. *The
    Diabetes Educator 31*(2) 225-234.

Vigersky, R.(2011). An overview of management issues in adult patients with Type 2
    Diabetes Mellitus *Journal of Diabetes Science and Technology 5*(2) 245-250.